Air Fryer R

Cookbook

Coloured Book with Traditional British Dishes for Beginners and Advanced Users

Maya Harrison

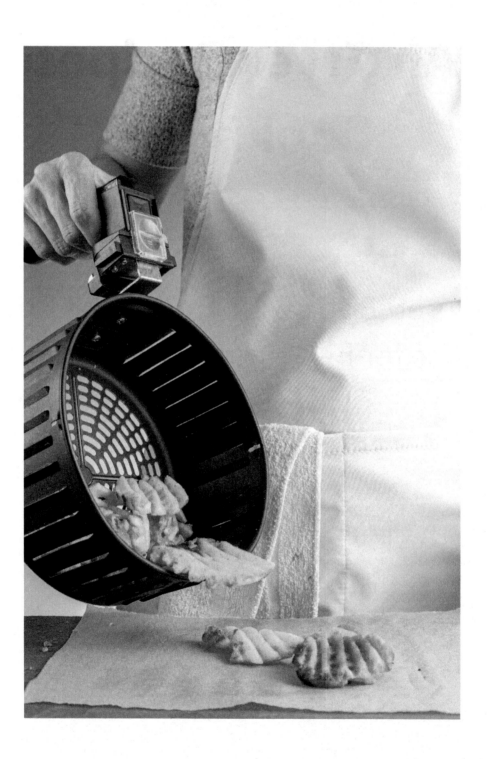

TABLE OF CONTENTS

INTRODUCTION

Air Fryers have started to become popular, due to the fact that you can avoid many of the unhealthy aspects of modern cooking. But what is an Air Fryer exactly, and how on earth does it work?

Air Fryers are basically an upgraded, enhanced countertop oven, but they became popular for one particular reason. In fact, many of the manufacturers, such as Philips, market this machine solely based on the claim that the Air Fryers accurately mimic deep-frying, which, although extremely unhealthy, is still very popular in this day and age (as it is, in my opinion, one of the most delicious ways to eat food).

Air Fryers work with the use of a fan and a heating mechanism. You place the food you want cooked in a basket or on the rack, turn on the machine, and the Air Fryer distributes oven-temperature hot air around your food. It provides consistent, pervasive heat evenly to all the food within. This heat circulation achieves the crispy taste and texture that is so tantalizing in deep fried foods, but without the unhealthy and dangerous oil! Both have been replaced by this miracle machine with hot air and a fan.

ADVANTAGES TO USING AN AIR FRYER

I may have already slipped in a few of the advantages to using an Air Fryer, but now let's expand a little more on everything an Air Fryer can do for you. After all, no investment should be made unless it's absolutely worthwhile.

And in truth, the Air Fryer is very worthwhile. I cannot begin to tell you how the advantages start piling up; this is not just another average appliance that everyone is getting because of a simple trend. People are getting Air Fryers because of their incredible, numerous, multifaceted benefits.

There are, however, a few notable advantages of using an Air Fryer, which I'll list below. If you don't know anything else about Air Fryers, I hope that these will convince you of their worth.

HEALTHIER COOKING

This is perhaps the top benefit that comes with air frying. In a society that really struggles with healthy cooking, we can use all the help we can get. Luckily, Air Fryers make it easy, all while maintaining many of the factors that make unhealthy food delicious!

Air Fryers use very little oil, which is one of the best ways to replace those unhealthy fried foods, like fried chicken, potatoes, and so many others. If you are like me (a lover of deep fried foods) then this is the answer to your dilemma of healthy eating while still enjoying the crispy taste of food!

Do keep in mind that you still need to spray fried foods, such as fish, with a touch of oil to make sure it does get evenly crispy. All in all, however, there is no denying the amount of oils is a whole lot less.

This singular change makes all the difference in the world. Healthy eating has never been easier, as you'll get the same crispy and flavoursome results, with minimal amounts of added oils. You'll even be able to "fry" foods you never were able to before—the possibilities are endless!

SAFER AND EASIER

Nothing scares me more than a hot pot of oil. It is an accident waiting to happen, and getting struck with burning oil splatters is no joke! But this, and its corresponding injuries, is often the price to pay for deep fried foods.

Air Fryers are also user-friendly, and this makes a huge difference. You don't have to feel like you are studying for a degree when working with an Air Fryer. Making dinner is far less complicated in an Air Fryer than many of the traditional methods of cooking. For some meals—unless you choose one of the more complex recipes I'll share later—you can even revert to placing a small piece of meat (even if it happens to be frozen!) into the basket and select the cooking settings.

The simplicity of the Air Fryer is its beauty. You will save countless time and unnecessary frustrations, and still make delicious food!

FASTER THAN COOKING IN THE OVEN

Once you buy an Air Fryer and set it to heat for the first time, you won't know what hit you! The average normal oven needs about 10 minutes to preheat. Due to the Air Fryer's smaller size and innovative design, it will be ready to go in no time!

It's even faster during the actual cooking. With the circulation that allows your food to be cooked crisp and even, it cuts a whole lot of cooking time out of the equation. This is amazing, especially in this day and age where technology, work, friends, family, and even pets are constantly demanding our attention.

Just imagine! You could set your food in the Air Fryer, and (with some recipes) it will be ready to eat in less than 20 minutes!

SAVES SPACE

If you are someone living in a small apartment, or a student accommodation, then an Air Fryer is perfect for you. Air Fryers are much smaller in comparison to a conventional oven and you can easily make use of this Air Fryer in 1 cubic foot of your kitchen.

You can even pack your Air Fryer away after use if need be, but the majority of people choose to keep it out on the counter. But it's nice to have the option to move your Air Fryer around if space becomes an issue.

LOW OPERATING COSTS

Considering how much cooking oil costs these days and the amount you need to use, you will soon be cutting costs in making deep fried foods. All an Air Fryer uses is a small amount of oil and some of the electricity to power up the Air Fryer, about the same amount that a countertop oven would.

Not only will you be cutting out the massive oil costs, which will save money, you will likely also save money by ordering out less, as you'll be able to replicate your favourite foods quickly and easily at home!

NO OIL SMELL

In reality, smelling like the food you just ate is not impressive, regardless of how delicious the food may be. This is what often happens, however, when people enjoy deep fried foods.

When deep frying foods, it also causes the whole house to smell, and as the oil splatters around, it can leave a massive mess. The oil can even harden on the walls, causing grime to build up into a nasty concentration of dirt and grease.

With less cooking oil, Air Fryers don't have any of those oil smells and keeps the space cleaner around you, as all the oils, smells, and actual cooking are contained within the machine.

PRESERVES NUTRIENTS

When you are cooking your food in an Air Fryer, it actually protects a lot of the food from losing all its moisture. This means that with the use of a little oil, as well as circulation with hot air, it can allow your food to keep most of its nutrients which is excellent for you!

If you want to cook healthy foods with the purpose of maintaining as many nutrients as possible, then an Air Fryer is perfect for you!

EASIER TO CLEAN

Cleaning is perhaps the bane of my existence, especially after cooking and having a long day. This can really take away a lot of the pleasure of making yourself a great meal. But an Air Fryer lightens the burden by being easy to clean!

Consistent cleaning after using it (much like any pot or pan) can allow for easier and simpler living. You just need some soapy water and a non-scratch sponge to clean both the exterior and the interior of your Air Fryer. Some Air Fryers are even dishwasher-safe!

GREAT FLAVOUR

The flavour of Air Fryer "fried" foods is nearly identical to traditional frying, and the texture is exact. You can cook a lot of those great frozen foods, such as onion rings or french fries, and still achieve that crunchy effect. This certainly can help you turn to healthier foods, especially if your goal is for healthy but quality meals.

The Air Fryer helps to cook your food to perfect crispness, instead of the soggy mess that happens when you try alternative methods of cooking foods that are meant to be deep fried (like chicken tenders). No one really enjoys mushy food. The Air Fryer keeps that desired element while remaining healthy.

All you will really need is just some cooking oil sprayed outside of your food to end up with a cooked interior and a crunchy exterior. So no worries! You still can eat your foods with a crunch and a healthier result!

VERSATILE

Unlike rice cookers meant just for rice, or bread makers meant just for bread, you will find that an Air Fryer leaves a lot of room to be both versatile and healthier. You can cook almost anything you would like in the Air Fryer (as long as it fits). From spaghetti squash, to desserts, even to fried chicken!
You will probably never run out of air frying options!

VARIOUS TYPES OF AIR FRYERS AND HOW TO CHOOSE THE ONE FOR YOU

There isn't one standardized choice of Air Fryers, which means you are far more likely to find an Air Fryer that really suits your particular needs. Whether it be size or price, you have a wider variety of choices than what normally comes with conventional ovens.

So what are the key aspects that you need to take into consideration when getting yourself a nice Air Fryer? Let's begin:

- **Dimensions:** Obviously they come in different sizes, and despite saving space, some can still be bulky. When thinking about your countertop, you do want to consider its size and dimensions. You don't want to play a game of tilt with your Air Fryer, nor have it taken up all the extra space you have!

- **Safety Features:** You may want to check that it has an auto shutoff, as it is certainly a desirable feature. Air Fryers can get very hot during use, and an auto-shutoff can save you a lot of stress and fire emergencies. Furthermore, having a cool exterior can prevent potential red and burnt hands. So do yourself a favour and make sure they have all these elements at hand.

- **Reviews:** Naturally, this is the best thing to check out. Considering that the businesses rarely give out all the information, you will certainly find it out when people leave reviews. The customer hides nothing, and if they are unhappy, they make sure everyone else knows about it. However, if people are very happy, many of them will also note it in the reviews, and it is best to target the Air Fryers that tend to have the high reviews.

TWO COMMON DIFFERENCES

Beyond those functional differences, there are two mainstream designs of Air Fryers: basket Air Fryers and oven Air Fryers. Each has very unique and distinguished features in which to enjoy. Let us take a look at the differences between the two:

BASKET AIR FRYERS

Basket fryers are known to need less space than oven Air Fryers, which is very practical if you have limited space. Not only does it save space, but it also saves time, as the food is quickly heated up (without unnecessarily heating up the kitchen). Unlike an oven Air Fryer, and the larger traditional oven, it only takes about 1-2 minutes for the basket Air Fryer to heat up, and it is quite easy to place the foods inside of the basket.

The cons are, for one, that it does make a lot more noise than the oven Air Fryer. You also will not be able to watch the food as it cooks, which can increase the chances of burnt food if you are not careful. Also, a basket Air Fryer may not be the best if you need to cook a lot of food, as it is limited in capacity. This means that batch cooking may be required if you need a large amount of food.

This makes a basket Air Fryer ideal if you have a limited budget, don't need to cook a huge amount of food, and have limited free time. They are quick, small, and convenient, especially perfect for people who are students or single working professionals, and maybe even you!

OVEN AIR FRYERS

Oven Air Fryers, in contrast, have a larger capacity, which means you can cook a lot more food at the same time. They also have multiple functions for cooking and cut down on the noise than the basket Air Fryer. You will also be able to move the food closer or even further away from the heating element. There is a lot more flexibility involved in the use of an oven Air Fryer. Best of all, you can place parts of the oven Air Fryer into the dishwasher to be washed (thus cutting down the cleaning process, if you happen to have a dishwasher).

But, do be aware that it takes up more counter space, and takes a larger initial bite out of your wallet. It may also heat up the kitchen more, and if you are in fashion and aesthetic design, it might be disappointing to find out the colours and themes are more limited than basket Air Fryers.

These are the two main common types of Air Fryers; however, there are new types of Air Fryers that are coming to light for you to use and enjoy, most notably, the paddle-type Air Fryer. This version has a paddle that moves through the basket of your Air Fryer in order to help circulate hot air in between each piece of food.

This saves you the effort of pulling your food out at a specific time and shaking or stirring it. These can also be noisy, and heat up the space, and are not small and convenient; however, if you are someone looking for convenience, then this is the Air Fryer to go for.

ACCESSORY TOOLS FOR AIR FRYER COOKING

I love how Air Fryers save time, so I've compiled a list of my favorite time-saving tools that I often use when meal prepping with my Air Fryer. Anything to help make your life easier and healthier should certainly be considered, and what better way to help than by adding some accessories to your Air Fryer inventory?

MANDOLINE

Preparation is always needed before jumping into air frying, and getting yourself the mandoline slicer is the perfect tool to slice online rings, pickles, or even the best and crunchiest chips. You can select the thickness or thinness, depending on what the recipe needs and says, so you will always be able to get the perfect crispness.

GRILL PAN

This is simply a pan created with a perforated surface. With this tool, you can both grill and sear foods like fish or even vegetables inside your Air Fryer. They are also commonly non-stick, which really helps your overall cleanup.

However, before you purchase a grill pan, make sure the Air Fryer model you have does support the grill pan. The last thing you want is to find that your grill pan just does not fit inside your Air Fryer.

HEAT RESISTANT TONGS

There is no denying how hot an Air Fryer can get inside, and unless you are a superhero, you will need some help manoeuvring in foods in and outside of the basket if need be. Using heat-resistant tongs can really make your life infinitely easier by keeping your foods, and your hands, safe. They are affordable, and really useful to allow for an even cooking process.

AIR FRYER LINERS

If you'd like to further decrease your clean-up time, then this is for you! These liners are both non-stick and non-toxic, making this a classic little investment for you to consider. They prevent the food from sticking to your Air Fryer and help in the process of keeping your little machine clean. You will not have to worry about burnt foods inside your fryer again!

AIR FRYER RACK

This adds a little bit more versatility as you can really take advantage of the surface cooking. With a rack, you ensure that heat is evenly distributed to all 360 degrees of your food. They are very safe and easy to use, and they increase the number of dishes you can cook at the same time

BAKING PANS

With an Air Fryer, you can even bake! You just need the right equipment, such as a barrel or round pan. With this you can even bake pizza, bread, muffins, and more. Imagine telling people you baked your own cake with an Air Fryer!

SILICONE BAKING CUPS

From egg bites to muffins, these are individual cups you can use in order to help compensate for the smaller space within an Air Fryer. The silicone material is heat-resistant, and allows for easier release of the contents, which spares you a lot of time cleaning. If you are a fan of baking, then this is a must have.

OIL SPRAYER

Naturally, one of the top benefits is needing much less oil when cooking with an Air Fryer, but it does not necessarily mean that you can cook with no oil at all. An oil sprayer is the key to getting the food you want to that nice golden-brown. You can use any oil that you like to use when cooking; all you need is a little spritz before you close the machine, and you are set!

THERMAPEN

Having the right cooking time is very important, but temperature also counts for a lot, and this is a nice little accessory to add to your collection. Having an instant-read thermometer can ensure all the food you have is cooked (and evenly so). If you are not completely certain at what temperatures food should be, you can always check out the various different guides.

HOW TO CLEAN AN AIR FRYER

As mentioned before, an Air Fryer is really easy to clean, but that doesn't mean you'll never need to clean it! Also, please remember that the cleanliness of your machine depends on how often you use it, and what you use it for.

It is recommended that you clean your Air Fryer after every use. As tempting as it may be to skip a day, it really is not worth it over the long run.
And that is the first step that comes with cleaning an Air Fryer:

- Do not delay the cleaning. Simply don't. Allowing crumbs or random bits of food to harden overnight can turn an easy task into a nightmare of a chore. If you do happen to air-fry foods that come with a form of sticky sauce, then the warmer they are, the easier again they will be to clean and remove.

- Unplug the machine, and use warm and soapy water to properly remove the dirt and components. You do not want anything abrasive in there. If there is food that gets stuck, try soaking it until it is soft enough to remove.

- If there is any food that happens to be stuck on the grate or in the basket, then you should consider gently using a toothpick or even a wooden skewer to scrape it off, in order to be thorough with your cleaning process.

- Remember to wipe the inside with a damp, soapy cloth, and remember to remove both the drawer and the basket.

- Finally, wipe the outside of your Air Fryer with a damp cloth or a sponge.

If there are any odors that seem to be stuck to your Air Fryer after cooking a strong food, even after you have cleaned it, then you can consider using a product called NewAir.

Just soak it in with water for about 3o minutes to an hour before you clean it. If the smell remains, then rub one lemon half over the drawer and the basket. Allow it to soak for another 30 minutes before washing it again.

Please do be careful with any non-stick appliances. They are a wonder for cleaning, but they can flake or come off over time. Be gentle, as you do not want anything to scratch or to even chip the coating. Not only does it ruin a little bit of the aesthetic look, a small part of your Air Fryer will constantly be struggling with sticky food.

There you have it! The first stepping stones and foundational knowledge of an Air Fryer. The device you will choose, and how you will use it is up to you, but there are still so many exciting varieties, choices, and options to come!

FRIED BACON

2 minutes

8 minutes

3

INGREDIENTS

- 1 pack Back Bacon

DIRECTIONS

1. Place the bacon slices in a single layer of the air fryer tray or in the basket.
2. Cook for 8 - 10 minutes at 200°C. There is no need to preheat
3. Depending on the thickness of the bacon the cooking time may vary, so check as you go along whether it is cooked to the point you want

Nutrition: Calories: 118kcal; Protein: 21g; Fat: 4g

SCOTCH EGGS

15 minutes

12 minutes

6

INGREDIENTS

- 6 boiled eggs peeled
- 1 packet 400g Powters Sausagemeat
- 30 g Flour
- ½ teaspoon garlic powder
- 1 large egg beaten
- 120 g Breadcrumbs
- 1 tablespoon brown sugar
- ½ smoked paprika

DIRECTIONS

1. Divide the sausage into 6 equal portions and roll them into a balls
2. Place a sausage ball on your counter or parchment paper if you don't want to clean up later.
3. Pat the sausage balls until they reach the form of an oval big enough to hold an egg.
4. Place the peeled, boiled eggs in the center of the sausages patties and wrap the sausages around the eggs, applying pressure with your hands.
5. Now take 3 bowls and put, in order: flour and garlic powder combined, beaten egg, panko or breadcrumbs with brown sugar and smoked paprika.
6. Roll each sausage-covered egg in bowl 1, then dip in bowl 2 and coat in the breadcrumbs bowl.
7. Preheat your air fryer to 190°C for 10 minutes.
8. Place Scotch eggs in the air fryer basket, ensuring enough space between each other to let the air circulate.
9. Air fry the eggs for 12 minutes, evenly turning halfway through to brown.

Nutrition: Calories 396; Fat 27 g; Protein 29 g; Carbs 16 g; Fibre 1 g; Sugar 1 g

WALNUT PANCAKE

10 minutes

20 minutes

4

INGREDIENTS

- 3 tbsp melted butter, divided
- 130 g flour
- 2 tbsp sugar
- 1½ tsp baking powder
- ¼ tsp salt
- 1 egg, beaten
- 95 ml milk
- 1 tsp pure vanilla extract
- 65 g roughly chopped walnuts
- Maple syrup or fresh sliced fruit, for serving

DIRECTIONS

1. Grease a baking pan with 1 tbsp of melted butter.
2. Mix together the flour, sugar, baking powder, and salt in a medium bowl. Add the beaten egg, the remaining 2 tbsp of melted butter, milk, and vanilla and stir until the batter is sticky but slightly lumpy.
3. Slowly pour the batter into the greased baking pan and scatter with the walnuts.
4. Place the pan on the bake position.
5. Select Bake, set temperature to 165°C, and set time to 20 min.
6. When cooked, the pancake should be golden brown and well cooked.
7. Let the pancake rest for 5 min and serve topped with maple syrup or fresh fruit, if desired.

Nutrition: Calories 271; Fat 14.5 g; Carbohydrates 22 g; Sugar 1.2 g; Protein 11 g

AIR FRYER BLACK PUDDING (PACKED)

0 minutes

9 minutes

2

INGREDIENTS

- Black Pudding Slices

DIRECTIONS

1. If your black pudding is still frozen, air fry it in the air fryer for 6 minutes at 80°C, then it will be soft enough to cut.
2. Remove from the air fryer. Cut into slices, removing the wrapper.
3. Place the slices in the frying basket and cook at 180°C for 9 minutes.
4. Serve.

Nutrition: Calories: 297kcal; Fat: 22 g

BANANA MUFFINS

5 minutes

15 minutes

12

INGREDIENTS

- 190g plain flour
- 90g granulated sugar
- 1 teaspoon baking powder
- 115g salted butter, melted
- 1 large egg
- 2 medium bananas, peeled and mashed
- 60g chopped pecans

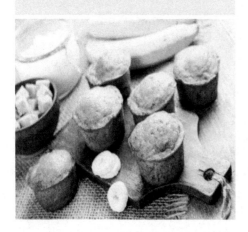

DIRECTIONS

1. Preheat the air fryer to 150°C.
2. In a large bowl, whisk the flour, sugar, and baking powder.
3. Add butter, egg, and bananas, and stir until well combined and thick.
4. Gently fold in pecans. Divide batter evenly among twelve silicone or aluminium muffin cups, filling cups about halfway full.
5. Place cups in the air fryer basket, working in batches as necessary. Cook them for 15 minutes until muffin edges are brown and a toothpick inserted into the centre comes out clean.
6. Let cool 5 minutes before serving.

Nutrition: Calories 169; Fat 8.5 g; Carbs 22 g; Fibre 1.5 g; Sugar 7 g; Protein 2.5 g

SAUSAGE AND CHEESE BALLS

 12 minutes

 12 minutes

 16

INGREDIENTS

- 450 g pork breakfast sausage
- 65 g shredded Cheddar cheese
- 30 g full-fat cream cheese, softened
- 1 large egg

DIRECTIONS

1. Mix all ingredients in a large bowl. Form into sixteen (2.5 cm) balls. Move the balls into the air fryer basket.
2. Set the temperature to 200°C and air fry for 12 min.
3. Shake the basket two- or three times during cooking. Sausage balls will now be browned on the outside and have an internal temperature of at least 63°C when thoroughly cooked.
4. Serve warm.

Nutrition: Calories: 424; Fat: 32g; Protein: 23g; Carbs: 2g; Fibre: 0g

CHOCOLATE SCONES

15 minutes

15 minutes

8

INGREDIENTS

- 115g cold salted butter, divided
- 250g plain flour
- 110g brown sugar
- ½ teaspoon baking powder
- 1 large egg
- 85g semisweet chocolate chips

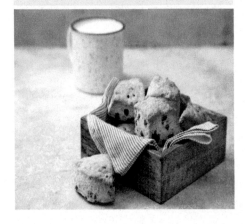

DIRECTIONS

1. Preheat the air fryer to 160°C. Cut parchment paper to fit the air fryer basket.
2. Chill 6 tablespoons butter in the freezer for 10 minutes.
3. Add the remaining butter to a small microwave-safe bowl, and microwave for 30 seconds until melted, and then set aside.
4. Mix the flour, brown sugar, and baking powder in a large bowl.
5. Remove butter from freezer and grate into the flour bowl. Use a wooden spoon to evenly distribute; add egg and buttermilk and stir gently until a sticky dough forms. Gently fold in chocolate chips.
6. Turn dough out onto a lightly floured surface. Fold a couple of times and gently form into a 15 cm round. Cut into eight triangles.
7. Place scones on parchment in the air fryer basket, leaving at least 5 cm space between each (you can cook in batches).
8. Brush each scone with melted butter, then cook them for 15 minutes until scones are dark golden brown and crispy on the edges, and a toothpick inserted into the centre comes out clean.
9. Serve warm.

Nutrition: Calories 304; Fat 12 g; Carbs 45.5 g; Fibre 1.5 g; Sugar 20.5 g; Protein 5 g

SAUSAGES IN AIR FRYER

5 minutes

12 minutes

6

INGREDIENTS

- 6 Sausages
- 3 squirts Spray Oil

DIRECTIONS

1. Preheat your air fryer to 180°C for 5 minutes
2. Prick each sausage a couple of times (you can use a knife or fork).
3. Spray the bottom of the air fryer with a few splashes of oil to prevent the sausages from sticking.
4. Use the tongs to gently insert the sausages (do not let them touch so that they cook evenly).
5. Set timer to 12 minutes (adjust the time for small, large or frozen sausages).
6. Halfway through cooking, turn with tongs.
7. Check after 12 minutes and reheat if necessary.Serve with your chosen meal

Nutrition: Calories: 209kcal; Carbohydrates: 2g; Protein: 11g; Fat: 17g

VEGETABLES BREAKFAST FRITTATA

5 minutes

10 minutes

2

INGREDIENTS

- Oil or butter to grease the pan
- 3 eggs
- 1/4 red pepper, diced
- 1/4 green pepper, diced
- 10 baby spinach leaves, chopped
- Handful of cheddar cheese, grated
- Salt and pepper to season, optional

DIRECTIONS

1. In a bowl, beat the eggs. Season with salt and pepper as needed. Grease a skillet with oil or butter and place it in the air fryer.
2. Switch to 180°C and heat for 1 minute. Add peppers and air fry for 3 minutes. Pour in the spinach and egg mixture. Sprinkle melted cheese on top.
3. Cook for another 6 minutes, making sure not to overcook halfway through.

Nutrition: Calories: 254; Fat: 15.5 g; Protein: 19 g; Carbs: 8.5 g; Fibre: 3.5 g; Sugar: 0.5 g

CHAPTER 2: SIDE DISHES AND SNACKS

YORKSHIRE PUDDINGS

1 hour

18 minutes

4

INGREDIENTS

- 1 egg
- 4 tbsp (70 g) flour
- 4 tbsp (80 ml) milk
- 4 tbsp (80 ml) water
- 1/4 tsp salt

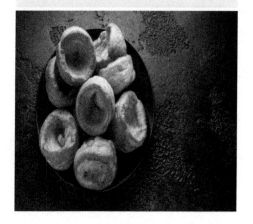

DIRECTIONS

1. Mix well all the ingredients together; you need to obtain a smooth batter with no lumps
2. Once the batter is ready, refrigerate for 30 to 60 minutes
3. Preheat the air fryer to 200 C
4. Grease a ramekin with some butter, then add a tsp of oil; heat at 200C in the air fryer for five minutes. This operation will prevent the batter from sticking
5. Once the ramekins are hot, add five tablespoons of Yorkshire Pudding mixture to each one
6. Cook at 200 C for 18 minutes
7. Do not open the air fryer while cooking!

Nutrition: Calories 89; Fat 2 g; Protein 4 g; Carbs 13 g; Fibre 2 g; Sugar 1 g

CREAMY MASHED POTATOES

5 minutes

25 minutes

4

INGREDIENTS

- 900 baking potatoes (small to medium)
- 40 g butter
- 60 g cream cheese
- 2 stalks of fresh chives
- salt and pepper to taste

DIRECTIONS

1. Start by placing your potatoes into a foil packet, Layout your foil, then place the potatoes in them.
2. Air fry for 25 minutes at 200C. Check after 25 minutes if they are soft; The actual time will depend on the type of air fryer you have and the size of the potatoes.
3. Use a fork (or a potato masher if you prefer) to mash the potatoes.
4. Put the potatoes in a bowl.
5. Add the cream cheese and butter.
6. Add the chives and continue to mix. Continue mixing until the potatoes are mashed and the cream cheese and butter are combined.
7. Plate, serve and enjoy!

Nutrition: Calories: 322; Sugar: 3 g; Fat: 11 g; Carbohydrates: 50 g; Fibre: 5 g; Protein: 7 g

ROASTED COURGETTE AND RED PEPPERS

5 minutes

15 minutes

6

INGREDIENTS

- 2 medium courgettes, cubed
- 1 red pepper, diced
- 2 garlic cloves, sliced
- 2 tablespoons olive oil
- ½ teaspoon salt

DIRECTIONS

1. Preheat the air fryer to 195°C.
2. Mix together the courgette, red pepper, and garlic with the olive oil and salt in a large bowl.
3. Transfer the mixture into the air fryer basket and roast for 7 minutes. Shake or stir, then roast for 7 to 8 minutes more.

Nutrition: Calories 55; Fat 5 g; Carbs 3 g; Fibre 1 g; Sugar 2 g; Protein 1 g

ASPARAGUS AND GREEN BEANS SALAD

15 minutes

6 minutes

3

INGREDIENTS

- 85 g asparagus, chopped
- 60 g green beans, chopped
- 130 g arugula, chopped
- 1 tbsp hazelnuts, chopped
- 1 tsp flax seeds
- 60 g Mozzarella, chopped
- 1 tbsp olive oil
- ½ tsp salt
- ½ tsp ground paprika
- ½ tsp ground black pepper
- Cooking Spray

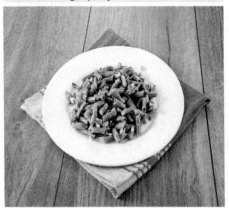

DIRECTIONS

1. Preheat the air fryer to 200°C. Put the asparagus and green beans in the air fryer and spray them with cooking spray. Cook the vegetables for 6 minutes at 200°C. Shake the vegetables after 3 minutes of cooking. Then cool them to room temperature and put them in the salad bowl.
2. Add hazelnuts, flax seeds, chopped Mozzarella, salt, ground paprika, and ground black pepper. Sprinkle the salad with olive oil and shake well.

Nutrition: Calories: 122; Fat: 9.4g; Fibre: 1.9g; Carbs: 4.3g; Protein:6.9g

PARMESAN AUBERGINE

| 15 minutes | 30 minutes | 4 |

INGREDIENTS

- 1 medium aubergine, peeled and cut into 1-cm-thick rounds
- 1 teaspoon salt, plus more for seasoning
- 60g plain flour
- 2 eggs
- 90g Italian bread crumbs
- 2 tablespoons grated Parmesan cheese
- Freshly ground black pepper
- Cooking oil spray
- 180g marinara sauce
- 40g shredded Parmesan cheese, divided
- 45g shredded mozzarella cheese, divided

DIRECTIONS

1. Preheat the air fryer to 200°C on Air Fry mode. Spray the air fryer basket with cooking oil.
2. Pat the aubergine dry with paper towels.
3. Beat the egg in a shallow bowl, add the flour to the second bowl, and mix the bread crumbs, Parmesan cheese, salt and pepper in the third bowl.
4. Dip each aubergine round in the flour, then in the eggs, and finally in the bread crumbs.
5. Working in batches, place the coated aubergine rounds in the basket (do not stack them), and spray them with the cooking oil.
6. Air Fry them for 10 minutes; after 7 minutes of cooking time, top each aubergine round with 1 teaspoon of marinara sauce, ½ tablespoon each of shredded Parmesan and mozzarella cheese, then resume cooking.
7. Do the same with the remaining aubergine rounds.
8. When done, serve immediately.

Nutrition: Calories 258; Fat 9 g; Carbs 30 g; Fibre 6 g; Sugar 8 g; Protein 15 g

MASHED POTATO PANCAKES

5 minutes

15 minutes

6

INGREDIENTS

- 250 g Mashed Potatoes
- 100 g cheddar cheese
- 1 green onion chopped
- 2 strips of cooked bacon
- 1 egg
- 2 tbsp flour
- 100 g panko bread crumbs
- Salt and Pepper to taste

DIRECTIONS

1. Mix Potatoes, egg, cheese,bacon, green onion, and flour
2. Make into a patty form.
3. Coat in panko bread crumbs
4. Place in the freezer for 10 minutes to hold form.
5. Place foil over your rack on your air fryer
6. Cook on 200 C for 10 minutes
7. Flip over and cook for an additional 5 minutes.

Nutrition: Calories: 273; Total Fat: 13g; Carbohydrates: 28g; Fibre: 2g; Sugar: 2g; Protein: 11g

COURGETTE AND POTATO TOTS

5 minutes

20 minutes

4

INGREDIENTS

- 1 large courgette, grated
- 1 medium baked potato, skin removed and mashed
- 30 g shredded Cheddar cheese
- 1 large egg, beaten
- 1/2 tsp kosher salt
- Cooking Spray

DIRECTIONS

1. Place the baking pan on the air fry position. Select Air Fry, set the temperature to 200°C, and set the time to 10 min.
2. Wrap now the grated courgette in a paper towel and squeeze out any excess liquid, then combine the courgette, baked potato, shredded Cheddar cheese, egg, and kosher salt in a large bowl.
3. Spray the baking pan with cooking spray, then place individual tablespoons of the courgette mixture in the pan. Air fry for 10 min. Repeat this process with the remaining mixture.
4. Remove the tots and allow to cool on a wire rack for 5 min before serving.

Nutrition: Calories 128; Fat 3.5 g; Carbohydrates 17 g; Protein 5.3 g; Fibre 2 g; Sugar 1.5 g

BRUSSELS SPROUTS IN AIR FRYER

20 minutes

5 minutes

5

INGREDIENTS

- 1/4 tsp. salt
- 1 tbsp. balsamic vinegar
- 1 tbsp. olive oil
- 400 g Brussels sprouts

DIRECTIONS

1. Cut Brussels sprouts in half lengthwise. Toss with salt, vinegar, and olive oil till coated thoroughly.
2. Add coated sprouts to air fryer, cooking 8-10 min at 200°C. Shake after 5 min of cooking.
3. Brussels sprouts are ready to devour when brown and crisp!

Nutrition: Calories 430; Fat 26.5 g; Carbohydrates 27.1 g; Sugar 0 g; Protein 16.7 g

LEMON AND BUTTER ARTICHOKE

5 minutes

15 minutes

4

INGREDIENTS

- 340 g artichoke hearts
- Juice of ½ lemon
- 4 tbsp butter, melted
- 2 tbsp tarragon, chopped
- Salt and black pepper to the taste

DIRECTIONS

1. In a bowl, mix all the ingredients, toss, transfer the artichokes to your air fryer's basket and cook at 185°C for 15 minutes.
2. Prepare the portions and serve them as a side dish.

Nutrition: Calories: 200; Fat: 7g; Fibre: 2g; Carbs: 3g; Protein:7 g

GOAT CHEESE CAULIFLOWER AND BACON

5 minutes

20 minutes

4

INGREDIENTS

- 1 Kg cauliflower florets, roughly chopped
- 4 bacon strips, chopped
- Salt and black pepper to the taste
- 65 g spring onions, chopped
- 1 tbsp garlic, minced
- 285 g goat cheese, crumbled
- 30 g soft cream cheese
- Cooking Spray

DIRECTIONS

1. Grease a baking pan that fits the air fryer with the cooking spray and mix all the ingredients except the goat cheese into the pan.
2. Sprinkle the cheese on top, introduce the pan to the air fryer and cook at 200°C for 20 minutes. Prepare the portions and serve them as a side dish.

Nutrition: Calories: 203; Fat: 13g; Fibre: 2g; Carbs: 5g; Protein:9g

CRISPY CHEESY ASPARAGUS

15 minutes

6 minutes

4

INGREDIENTS

- 2 egg whites
- 30 ml water
- 30 g + 2 tbsp of grated Parmesan cheese, divided
- 90 g panko breadcrumbs
- 1/4 tsp salt
- 340 g of fresh asparagus spears, ends trimmed
- Cooking Spray

DIRECTIONS

1. In a shallow dish, whisk together egg whites, water, until slightly foamy. Thoroughly combine 30 g of Parmesan cheese, breadcrumbs, and salt in a separate shallow dish.
2. Dip now the asparagus in the egg white, then roll in the cheese mixture to coat well.
3. Place the asparagus in the air fry basket in a single layer, leaving space between each spear. Spritz the asparagus with cooking spray.
4. Place the basket in the air fry position.
5. Select Air Fry, set the temperature to 200°C, and set the time to 6 min.
6. When cooking is done, the asparagus should be golden brown and crisp. Remove the basket from the air fryer grill. Sprinkle with the remaining 2 tbsp of cheese and serve hot.

Nutrition: Calories 130; Fat 1.3 g; Carbohydrates 22 g; Protein 6.8 g; Fibre 2.5 g; Sugar 3 g

CHUNKY CHIPS IN AIR FRYER

12 minutes

30 minutes

3

INGREDIENTS

- 4 Medium Potatoes Maris Piper or King Edwards
- 1 tbsp Rapeseed Oil or Canola / Vegetable / Olive Oil
- Salt to taste
- Pepper to taste

DIRECTIONS

1. Peel the potatoes - this is optional and can be cooked with the skins on. Cut the potato lengthwise into 2-3 pieces (depending on the size of the potato!)
2. Rinse or soak in cold water to remove starch.
3. Put the potatoes in a pot and pour cold water into it and bring to boil. After boiling for 5-7 minutes they should be soft enough to pierce with a fork. Do not overheat or they will fall apart.
4. Place the boiled potatoes on a wire rack using a slotted spoon. Allow to air dry while preheating the air fryer.
5. Preheat air fryer to 200°C
6. Brush them with oil.
7. Place in the air fryer and air fry for 15-20 minutes
8. Add your desired amount of salt and pepper.
9. Serve!

Nutrition: Calories: 378; Fat 4 g; Protein 10 g; Carbs 85 g; Fibre 10 g; Sugar 4 g;

CHAPTER 3: POULTRY RECIPES

TANDOORI CHICKEN TIKKA KEBAB

10 minutes

15 minutes

6

INGREDIENTS

- 2-3 Large Chicken Breast Cubed
- 4 tbsp Fat Free Yoghurt (or full fat)
- 2 tbsp Tandoori Masala Spice Blend Powder (or Garam Masala)
- 2 cloves Garlic Crushed
- 1 Lemon ½ for the juice, ½ sliced into wedges to serve
- Spray oil

Equipment
- Wooden Kebab Sticks

DIRECTIONS

1. When preparing chicken, it is best to soak the bamboo skewers in water. Cut them according to the size of the pan or tray you will be cooking with.
2. In a bowl or food bag, put the yoghurt, tandoori masala, garlic and the juice of half a lemon. Add the diced chicken breast and mix. For best results, let it marinate for two hours in the refrigerator. Thread the chicken onto kebab sticks. 4-6 chicken sticks are needed.
3. Preheat to 180°C for 5 minutes, add oil and fry for about 15 minutes. It is not necessary to flip halfway through cooking.

Optional: Sprinkle finely chopped coriander on top when serving.

Nutrition: Calories: 107; Carbohydrates: 4 g; Protein: 17 g; Fat: 2 g Fibre: 1 g; Sugar: 1 g

WHOLE ROAST CHICKEN

5 minutes

1 hour

4

INGREDIENTS

- 1 whole chicken (up to 2kg, depending on the size of your air fryer)
- 1tbsp olive oil
- 1tsp smoked paprika
- 1tsp dried mixed herbs
- 1tsp garlic granules/salt

DIRECTIONS

1. Brush the chicken with olive oil using a brush. Mix the spices and sprinkle them over the chicken. If it is not enough to cover the whole chicken, add more spice mix.
2. Place the chicken in the fryer basket with the breast side down. Bake at 180°C for 45 minutes. Check once or twice that it is well cooked and not burnt.
3. After 45 minutes, turn the chicken so that the breast is facing upwards. Bake another 15 minutes.
4. Make sure the chicken is well cooked. You can pierce it with a sharp knife to see if the juices run clear. If it is not cooked, put it back in the fryer and heat it up some more, checking from time to time.

Nutrition: Calories: 390; Fat: 24 g; Carbohydrates: 1 g; Fibre: 0 g; Sugar: 0 g; Protein: 41 g

THYME CHICKEN TENDERS

10 minutes

12 minutes

4

INGREDIENTS

- 450g boneless, skinless chicken tenders
- 2 teaspoons paprika
- 1 teaspoon garlic powder
- 1 teaspoon salt
- ½ teaspoon cayenne pepper
- ½ teaspoon dried thyme
- ½ teaspoon ground black pepper

DIRECTIONS

1. Preheat the air fryer to 200°C.
2. Place chicken tenders into a large bowl.
3. Mix paprika, garlic powder, salt, cayenne, thyme, and black pepper in a small bowl. Mix the spice mixture with the chicken and then toss to coat. Spritz the chicken with cooking spray.
4. Place the prepared chicken in your air fryer basket and cook for 12 minutes, turning halfway through the cooking time until the chicken is brown at the edges and the internal temperature reaches at least 75°C.
5. Serve warm.

Nutrition: Calories 205; Fat 7 g; Carbs 25 g; Fibre 2.5 g; Sugar 6 g; Protein 11 g

BACON-WRAPPED CHICKEN BREASTS

10 minutes

15 minutes

4

INGREDIENTS

- 30 g chopped fresh chives
- 2 tbsp lemon juice
- 1 tsp dried sage
- 1 tsp fresh rosemary leaves
- 65 g fresh parsley leaves
- 4 cloves garlic, peeled
- 1 tsp ground fennel
- 3 tsps. sea salt
- 1/2 tsp red pepper flakes
- 4 (115 g) skinless, boneless, chicken breasts, pounded 6.5 mm thick
- 8 slices bacon
- Sprigs of fresh rosemary, for garnish
- Cooking Spray

DIRECTIONS

1. Spritz the air fry basket with cooking spray.
2. Put the chives, garlic, fennel, salt, lemon juice, rosemary, parsley, sage, and red pepper flakes in a food processor, then pulse to purée until smooth.
3. Unfold the chicken breasts on a clean work surface, then brush the top side of the chicken breasts with the sauce.
4. Roll the chicken breasts up from the shorter side, then wrap each chicken roll with 2 bacon slices to cover. Secure with toothpicks.
5. Arrange the rolls in the air fry basket.
6. Place the basket on the air fry position.
7. Select Air Fry. Set temperature to 170°C and set time to 10 min. Flip the rolls halfway through.
8. After 10 min, increase the temperature to 200°C and set the time to 5 min.
9. When the cooking is done, the bacon should be browned and crispy.
10. Transfer the rolls to a large plate. Discard the toothpicks and spread with rosemary sprigs before serving.

Nutrition: Calories 221; Fat 11 g; Carbohydrates 1.25 g; Protein 31 g; Fibre 0.5 g; Sugar 0 g

CRISPY CHICKEN NUGGETS

10 minutes

8 minutes

4-5

INGREDIENTS

- 3 to 4 boneless chicken breasts
- 4 tbsp butter or 3 to 4 beat eggs, (approx)
- 100 g breadcrumbs, (approx)
- seasoning or spices of your choice, salt, pepper, paprika etc

DIRECTIONS

1. Cut chicken breasts up into small chunks (nuggets size).
2. Melt the butter in the microwave. Place the breadcrumbs in a bowl. You can buy bread crumbs, or if you have a few slices of bread, you can do it by yourself breaking them into crumbs (you can pulse the bread to turn it into crumbs using a blender).
3. Then, first dip the chicken in the melted butter (or beaten eggs if using beaten eggs instead), then roll in the bread crumbs.
4. Repeat with each chicken chunks and then place them in your air fryer basket. Depending on the air fryer's size, you may need to cook in two batches.
5. Cook at 200°C for 8 minutes. Check to see if it's fully cooked before serving.

Nutrition: Calories: 555; Fat: 33 g; Protein: 48 g; Carbs: 12 g; Fibre: 0.5 g; Sugar: 1 g

CHICKEN WINGS IN AIR FRYER

5 minutes

25 minutes

4

INGREDIENTS

- 1 kg chicken wings
- 1 tbsp olive oil
- ½ tsp garlic powder
- ½ tsp onion powder
- ½ tsp paprika
- ½ tsp salt
- ½ tsp black pepper

DIRECTIONS

1. Preheat the air fryer to 180°C. First, dry the chicken wings with a paper towel.
2. Place the chicken wings in a large bowl, cover with olive oil and toss the wings to coat as much as possible. Add all the spices and coat all the wings.
3. Place the chicken wings in the air fryer. Depending on the number of wings to be cooked and the size of the air fryer, it may be necessary to do this in batches. You can also use the air fryer's rack to hold more, but above all make sure that the wings do not touch each other and that they have room to crisp up.
4. Cook for about 20 minutes, turning 2-3 times to ensure even cooking. Increase the temperature to 200°C and bake for a further 5 minutes or until the skin is crispy.
5. Serve with BBQ sauce, chilli sauce or Buffalo sauce.

Nutrition: Calories: 853; Fat: 64 g; Carbohydrates: 25 g; Fibre: 1 g; Sugar: 1 g; Protein: 42 g

BBQ CHEDDAR STUFFED CHICKEN BREASTS

15 minutes

35 minutes

2

INGREDIENTS

- 3 strips bacon
- 2 (110 g) chicken breast skinless and boneless
- 60 g cheddar cheese, cubed
- 30 g BBQ sauce
- 1 pinch of salt and black pepper

DIRECTIONS

1. Place 1 strips of bacon in a crisper tray and air fry for 2 minutes. Cut the bacon into small pieces.
2. Line the crisper tray with parchment paper.
3. Make a horizontal 2.5 cm cut on the chicken to create an internal pouch.
4. Stuff each chicken breast with cooked bacon and cheese mixture, and then wrap the breasts with bacon.
5. Cover the chicken with BBQ sauce and place them on the lined tray.
6. Set the temperature of the Air Fryer to 195°C and the time for 20 minutes.
7. Turn the chicken breasts halfway through cooking time. When fully cooked, the chicken's internal temperature should be 75°C. Serve.

Nutrition: Calories: 375; Fat: 19 g; Carbs: 12.3 g; Sugar: 0 g; Protein:38 g

TENDER SPICY CHICKEN

1-3 hours

20 minutes

4

INGREDIENTS

- 455 g chicken breasts, boneless, skinless
- 65 g rice wine
- 1 tbsp stone-ground mustard
- 1 tsp garlic, minced
- 1 tsp black peppercorns, whole
- 1 tsp chili powder
- 1/4 tsp of sea salt and more to taste

DIRECTIONS

1. Place the chicken, wine, mustard, garlic, and whole peppercorns in a ceramic bowl. Seal the bowl and let the chicken marinate as long as you can in your refrigerator (ideal for about 3 hours).
2. Discard the marinade and place the chicken breasts in the Air Fryer cooking basket.
3. Cook the chicken breasts at 195°C for 12 min, turning them over halfway through the cooking time.
4. Season now the chicken with chili powder and salt. Serve immediately and enjoy!

Nutrition: Calories 404; Fat 29g; Carbohydrates 36g; Sugars 7g; Protein 24g

CHICKEN PARMESAN IN AIR FRYER

10 minutes

14 minutes

4

INGREDIENTS

- 2 large boneless chicken breasts
- Salt
- Freshly ground black pepper
- 40 g plain flour
- 2 large eggs
- 100 g panko bread crumbs
- 25 g freshly grated Parmesan
- 1 tsp. dried oregano
- 1/2 tsp. garlic powder
- 1/2 tsp. chilli flakes
- 240 g marinara/tomato sauce
- 100 g grated mozzarella
- Freshly chopped parsley, for garnish

DIRECTIONS

1. Gently butterfly the chicken, cutting in half widthwise to obtain 4 thin chicken pieces. Season with salt and pepper on both sides.
2. Place the flour in a shallow bowl and season with a large pinch of salt and pepper. Put the eggs in a second bowl and beat them. In a third bowl, mix together the breadcrumbs, parmesan cheese, oregano, garlic powder, and chilli flakes.
3. Working with chicken pieces one at a time, coat them in flour, then dip them in the eggs and finally press them into the panko mixture, being careful to coat both sides well.
4. Working in batches as needed, place the chicken in the basket and air fry at 200°C for 5 minutes per side. Top chicken with sauce and mozzarella and cook at 200°C for a further 3 minutes or until cheese is melted and golden.
5. Garnish with parsley to serve.

Nutrition: Calories: 419.5; Fat: 16 g; Protein: 30 g; Carbs: 32 g; Fibre: 3 g; Sugar: 10 g

SIMPLE HAMBURGERS

5 minutes

15 minutes

4

INGREDIENTS

- 500 g minced beef
- Salt
- Pepper

DIRECTIONS

1. Preheat Air Fryer to 200°C.
2. Divide minced beef into 4 equal portions and form them into burgers with your hands.
3. Season with salt, pepper, to your taste.
4. Air fry for 10 minutes.
5. Flip your burgers over, cook for a further 3 minutes.

Nutrition: Calories: 247.5; Fat: 15 g; Protein: 24 g; Carbs: 0 g; Fibre: 0 g; Sugar: 0 g

PORK RIBS WITH MARINADE

 10 minutes

 40 minutes

 4

INGREDIENTS

- 1 teaspoon smoked paprika
- 1 teaspoon garlic powder
- 1 teaspoon dark brown sugar
- ½ teaspoon ground mustard
- 1 teaspoon salt
- ½ teaspoon ground black pepper
- 2 tablespoons water
- 2 tablespoons olive oil
- 900g country-style pork ribs

DIRECTIONS

1. Combine smoked paprika, garlic powder, brown sugar, ground mustard, salt, and pepper in a small bowl.
2. Preheat the air fryer at 175°C for 3 minutes. Lightly grease the air fryer basket with cooking oil. Add water to bottom of air fryer.
3. Massage olive oil into pork ribs, and season ribs with spice mixture.
4. Add pork to air fryer basket, and cook them for 40 minutes, flipping every 10 minutes.
5. Transfer cooked pork to a serving platter and serve warm.

Nutrition: Calories 389; Fat 20 g; Carbs 3 g; Fibre 0.5 g; Sugar 2 g; Protein 48 g

BEEF TENDERLOIN IN AIR FRYER

 15 minutes

 15 minutes

 8

INGREDIENTS

- 900 g beef tenderloin
- 1 tbsp. vegetable oil
- 1 tbsp. dried oregano
- 1 tbsp. salt
- 1/2 tbsp. black pepper, cracked

DIRECTIONS

1. Pat dries tenderloin with paper towel and places it on a platter.
2. Drizzle vegetable oil and sprinkle oregano, salt, and pepper. Rub the spices on the meat until well coated.
3. Use the air fry setting and cook at 200°C for 22 min. After 22 minutes lower the temperature to 180°C and cook for 10 min.
4. Place the meat on a plate and allow to rest while tented with paper foil for 10 min before serving.

Nutrition: Calories 235; Fat 10.6 g; Carbohydrates 0.2 g; Sugar 0 g; Protein 32.4 g

WORCESTERSHIRE PORK TENDERLOIN

10 minutes

16 minutes

2

INGREDIENTS

- 1 tablespoon smoked paprika
- 2 teaspoons ground cumin
- 1 teaspoon garlic powder
- 1 teaspoon onion powder
- ¼ teaspoon cayenne pepper
- 1 teaspoon salt
- ½ teaspoon freshly ground black pepper
- 1 teaspoon Italian seasoning
- 2 tablespoons butter, melted
- 1 teaspoon Worcestershire sauce
- 1 (450g) pork tenderloin, halved crosswise

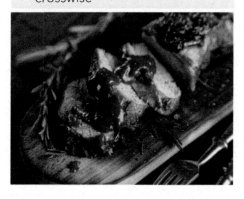

DIRECTIONS

1. Combine the paprika, cumin, garlic powder, onion powder, cayenne pepper, salt, black pepper, and Italian seasoning in a small bowl. Set aside.
2. Heat your air fryer at 175°C for 3 minutes in advance.
3. Whisk together the butter and Worcestershire sauce in a separate small bowl. Brush over the pork tenderloin halves, then rub with seasoning mix.
4. Place the pork in an air fryer basket lightly greased with olive oil and cook for 8 minutes, then flip. Cook an additional 8 minutes, then, using a meat thermometer, ensure the internal temperature is at least 60°C.
5. Let the pork tenderloin rest for 5 minutes before slicing and serving warm on a cutting board.

Nutrition: Calories 376; Fat 18 g; Carbs 7 g; Fibre 2 g; Sugar 1 g; Protein 45 g

COTTAGE PIE

15 minutes

40 minutes

4

INGREDIENTS

For the base:
- 300g minced beef
- 4 tbsp onions (coarsely diced)
- 2 tbsp carrots (coarsely diced)
- 4 mushrooms (soaked & diced)
- 4 cloves garlic (minced)
- 1 tsp dried mixed herbs
- 2 bay leaves
- 150 ml beef stock
- 1 tbsp Bovril
- 1 tsp ground black pepper
- 2 tbsp plain flour
- 30g butter

For the potato topping:
- 400g potatoes (quartered)
- 130 ml milk
- 2 tbsp butter
- Pinch of salt

Final egg wash topping:
- 1 egg yolk (beaten)

DIRECTIONS

1. Add 1 teaspoon of salt to a saucepan of water and bring to a boil before adding the potatoes. Cook the potatoes until very tender(15-17 minutes).
2. Melt the butter on the baking tray while preheating the fryer. Everything is prepared on the baking tray at 180 degrees C for this recipe.
3. Fry the onion for 1 minute, then add the garlic and fry for another minute until fragrant.
4. Add the ground beef, carrots, mushrooms, herb mix, black pepper, and bay leaves, mix well and cook for 20 minutes. Stir well every 5 minutes.
5. After 10 minutes, add Bovril and beef broth and stir. Continue stirring every 5 minutes.
6. Sprinkle all-purpose flour into the mixture and mix well 2-3 minutes before the end of the cooking time.
7. Hold the baking tray in the air fryer (to keep it warm) while you mash the potatoes.
8. Add the butter, salt, and milk (a little at a time) to the potatoes, mash, and mix well.
9. Spread mashed potatoes over the meat mixture, leveling with the back of a spoon.
10. Use a fork to draw lines across mashed potatoes, then pour the egg yolk on top.
11. Return the baking tray to the air fryer and cook at 180°C for 20 minutes.
12. Serve warm

Nutrition: Calories 360; Fat 22 g; Protein 19 g; Carbs 20 g; Fibre 2.5 g; Sugar 3 g

CHEESY BEEF MEATBALLS

5 minutes

18 minutes

2-3

INGREDIENTS

- 455 g ground beef
- 65 g grated Parmesan cheese
- 1 tbsp minced garlic
- 65 g Mozzarella cheese
- 1 tsp freshly ground pepper

DIRECTIONS

1. Place the crisper tray on the air fry position. Select Air Fry, set temp to 200°C and set the time to 18 min.
2. Get a bowl and combine all the ingredients in it.
3. Roll the meat mixture into 5 meatballs. Transfer to the crisper tray.
4. Air fry for 18 min.
5. Serve immediately.

Nutrition: Calories 176.5; Fat 11.5 g; Carbohydrates 0.2 g; Protein 16.5 g; Fibre 0 g; Sugar 0 g

ROAST BEEF

5 minutes

35 minutes

8

INGREDIENTS

- 1 Kg Beef Roast (up to 1.5 Kg)
- 1 tbsp Olive Oil
- Seasoning to taste

DIRECTIONS

1. Tie the roast to make it more compact
2. Rub the roast with oil
3. Add any seasonings you like
4. Place the beef in the air fryer basket
5. Air fry at 180°C for about 15 minutes per half of Kg (for medium rare beef).
6. Let the roast rest for 5 minutes and serve

Notes

Rare: 46 to 49°C (50 final temperature)

Medium-Rare: 50 to 55°C (58 final temperature)

Medium: 58 to 60°C (63 final temperature)

Medium-Well: 60 to 63°F (65 final temperature)

Well-Done: 65 to 69°F (72 final temperature)

Nutrition: Calories: 443; Fat: 29 g; Carbohydrates: 0 g; Fibre: 0 g; Sugar: 0 g; Protein: 43 g

BEEF WELLINGTON

15 minutes

35 minutes

8

INGREDIENTS

- 1kg beef fillet (one large piece)
- Chicken pate
- 2 sheets of short crust pastry
- 1 egg, beaten
- Salt
- Pepper

DIRECTIONS

1. Season the beef with salt, pepper and wrap tightly in cling film
2. Place the beef in the refrigerator for at least one hour
3. Roll out the pastry and brush the edges with the beaten egg
4. Spread the pate over the pastry, making sure it is distributed equally
5. Take now the beef out of the refrigerator and remove the cling film
6. Place the beef in the middle of your pastry
7. Wrap your pastry around the meat and seal the edges with a fork
8. Place in the Air Fryer and cook at 160°C for 35 minutes

Nutrition: Calories: 509; Fat: 28 g; Protein: 34 g; Carbs: 28 g; Fibre: 1 g; Sugar: 0.5 g

LAMB STEAKS

5 minutes

10 minutes

4

INGREDIENTS

- 4 Lamb Steaks
- 1 tsp. Frozen Chopped Garlic
- 2 tsp. Extra Virgin Olive Oil
- 2 tsp. Lemon Juice
- 2 tsp. Honey
- 1 tsp. Thyme
- Salt & Pepper
- Fresh Mint

DIRECTIONS

1. Place the lamb steaks on a chopping board, season with salt, pepper and dried thyme.
2. Thinly chop two tablespoons of mint and load into a bowl with everything except the lamb. Mix well then spoon over the lamb steaks. Place the steaks into the fridge for an hour, allow to marinate.
3. Place the steaks into the Air Fryer basket, add extra mint.
4. Air fry 10 minutes, 180°C.

Nutrition: Calories: 274.5; Fat: 19 g; Protein: 21g; Carbs: 4 g; Fibre: 0 g; Sugar: 4 g

CHAPTER 5: FISH AND SEAFOOD

COD WITH BUTTER AND LEMON

5 minutes

10 minutes

4

INGREDIENTS

- 4 (125g each) Fresh Cod loins (or fillets as you like)
- 30 g melted unsalted butter
- 1 Lemon sliced
- Salt to taste
- black pepper to taste

DIRECTIONS

1. Preheat the fryer to 200°C for 5 minutes.
2. Dry the cod fillets. Season the fish generously with salt and black pepper, then brush with the melted butter (just on one side of the fish)
3. Spray the frying basket with cooking oil. Place the cod fillets/loins in the basket, buttered side down, taking care that they do not touch each other. Brush the remaining butter over the fish, add a lemon slice to each fillet.
4. Cook for 10 minutes, carefully remove the fish and place on a plate.
5. Serve with lemon butter sauce, roast potatoes and vegetables and enjoy!

Nutrition: Calories: 85; Carbohydrates: 3 g; Protein: 1 g; Fat: 6 g; Fibre: 1 g; Sugar: 1 g

FISH AND CHIPS

8 minutes

12 minutes

2

INGREDIENTS

- 130 g all-purpose flour, divided
- 1 tbsp cornstarch
- 1/4 tsp baking soda
- 80 ml room temperature beer or water
- 1 egg
- 1/2 tsp salt
- 1/2 tsp black pepper
- 1/2 tsp paprika
- 1/4 tsp garlic powder
- 340 g cod filets, thawed
- Cooking spray

DIRECTIONS

1. Preheat air fryer to 200 C, air fryer setting. In a medium bowl, whisk together half the flour, cornstarch, baking soda, beer or water, and egg until smooth. Set aside.
2. Whisk together the remaining flour, salt, black pepper, paprika, and garlic powder in another medium bowl.
3. Dip the cod, piece by piece, into the batter. Drain excess and coat in the flour mixture. Spray the air fryer basket well with cooking spray or use a piece of parchment paper. Place the fish in the basket, ensuring the pieces don't touch each other.
4. Spray the fish too with a little of cooking spray.
5. Air fry for 10 to 12 minutes at 200 C. Halfway through cooking, spray again with more cooking spray. Turning is not necessary. It's ready when the fish is golden.
6. Sprinkle with a bit of salt if you like.
7. Arrange, serve and enjoy! You can serve with French fries, lemon wedges and tartar sauce for dipping.

Nutrition: Calories 417; Fat 4 g; Carbohydrates 52 g; Protein 40 g; Fibre 2 g; Sugar 1 g

SPICED TUNA STEAKS

5 minutes

9 minutes

4

INGREDIENTS

- 1 teaspoon garlic powder
- ½ teaspoon salt
- ¼ teaspoon dried thyme
- ¼ teaspoon dried oregano
- 4 tuna steaks
- 2 tablespoons olive oil
- 1 lemon, quartered

DIRECTIONS

1. Preheat the air fryer to 195°C.
2. Mix the garlic powder, salt, thyme, and oregano in a small bowl.
3. Coat the tuna steaks with olive oil, and season them with seasoning blend on both sides.
4. Place the tuna steaks in the air fryer basket in a single layer. 5. Cook the tuna steaks for 9 minutes; after 5 minutes of cooking time, flip them, and then resume cooking.
5. Serve warm.

Nutrition: Calories 269; Fat 9 g; Carbs 2 g; Fibre 0 g; Sugar 1 g; Protein 44 g

FAST BACON-WRAPPED SCALLOPS

5 minutes

15 minutes

4

INGREDIENTS

- 8 slices bacon, cut in half
- 16 sea scallops, patted dry
- Cooking Spray
- Salt, freshly ground black pepper, to taste
- 16 toothpicks, soaked for at least 30 min

DIRECTIONS

1. On a clean work surface, wrap half of a bacon slice around each scallop and secure with a toothpick.
2. Lay the bacon-wrapped scallops in the air fry basket in a single layer.
3. Spritz the scallops with cooking spray and sprinkle the salt and pepper to season.
4. Place the basket on the air fry position.
5. Select Air Fry, set the temperature to 190°C, and set the time to 10 min. Flip the scallops halfway through the cooking time.
6. When cooking is done, bacon should be cooked through, and the scallops should be firm. Remove the scallops from the air fryer grill to a plate Serve warm.

Nutrition: Calories 125.5; Fat 8 g; Carbohydrates 4 g; Protein 9 g; Fibre 1 g; Sugar 3 g

FISH PITAS WITH YOGURT

10 minutes

15 minutes

4

INGREDIENTS

- 455g pollock fillets, cut into 2cm pieces
- 60ml olive oil
- 1 teaspoon salt
- ½ teaspoon dried oregano
- ½ teaspoon dried thyme
- ½ teaspoon garlic powder
- ¼ teaspoon cayenne
- 4 whole wheat pitas
- 30g shredded lettuce
- 2 Roma tomatoes, diced
- Non-fat plain Greek yogurt
- Lemon, quartered

DIRECTIONS

1. Preheat the air fryer to 195°C.
2. Combine the pollock with olive oil, salt, oregano, thyme, garlic powder, and cayenne in a medium bowl.
3. Put the pollock into the air fryer basket and roast them for 15 minutes.
4. Serve inside pitas with lettuce, tomato, and Greek yogurt with a lemon wedge on the side.

Nutrition: Calories 279; Fat 15 g; Carbs 20 g; Fibre 3 g; Sugar 2.5 g; Protein 18 g

CRAB CAKES

20 minutes

15 minutes

4

INGREDIENTS

For The Crab Cakes:
- Cooking spray
- Hot sauce, for serving
- Lemon wedges, for serving
- 60 g of mayonnaise
- 1 egg
- 2 tsp. of cajun seasoning
- 1 tsp. of lemon zest
- 1/2 tsp. of salt
- 450 g of jumbo lump crab meat
- 120 g of Cracker crumbs (from about 20 crackers)
- 2 tbsp. of chives, finely chopped
- 2 tsp. of Dijon mustard

For The Tartar Sauce:
- 1/4 tsp. of Dijon mustard
- 1 tsp. of fresh dill, finely chopped
- 60 g of mayonnaise
- 80 g dill pickle, finely chopped
- 2 tsp. of capers, finely chopped
- 1 tsp. of fresh lemon juice
- 1 tbsp. of shallot, finely chopped

DIRECTIONS

1 Take a large bowl, whisk together egg, mayo, chives, Dijon mustard, lemon zest, cajun seasoning, and salt. Fold in crab meat and cracker crumbs.
2 Divide your mixture to form 8 patties.
3 Heat your Air Fryer to 190°C, spray the basket and the tops of your cakes with some cooking spray. Arrange the cakes into the basket in a single layer. Cook until crisp and deep golden brown, 12-14 minutes, flip halfway through.
4 Take a bowl and mix all of the tartar sauce ingredients.
5 Serve the cakes warm with lemon wedges, hot sauce and tartar sauce.

Nutrition: Calories: 265; Fat: 8 g; Protein: 24.5 g; Carbs: 21 g; Fibre: 1 g; Sugar: 0 g

TUNA PATTIES

9 minutes

15 minutes

10

INGREDIENTS

- 425 g canned albacore tuna, drained or 454g fresh tuna, diced
- 2-3 large eggs
- zest of 1 medium lemon
- 1 tbsp. lemon juice
- 1/4 tsp of **Kosher salt** , or to taste
- 55 g of breadcrumbs
- 1/2 tsp dried herbs (oregano, dill, basil, thyme or any combo)
- fresh cracked black pepper
- 3 tbsp grated parmesan cheese
- 1 stalk celery, finely chopped
- *Optional: tarter sauce, ranch, mayo, lemon slices*
- 3 tbsp minced onion
- 1/2 tsp garlic powder

DIRECTIONS

1. Take a medium bowl, mix the lemon zest, eggs, lemon juice, breadcrumbs, celery, parmesan cheese, onion, dried herbs, garlic powder, salt, pepper. Now stir well. Gently fold in the tuna.
2. Take your Air Fryer perforated baking paper, lay it inside the base of the Air Fryer. Now lightly spray the paper.
3. Try to keep all patties same size and thickness. Scoop 1/4 cup of the mixture, shape into patties about 8 cm wide x 1.3 cm thick and lay them inside the basket. Makes about 10 patties.
4. If patties are too soft, chill them for 1 hour or until firm. Brush the top of the patties with oil. Air Fry 185°C, 10 minutes, flip halfway through. After you flip the patties, spray the tops again.
5. Serve with your sauce and lemon slices.

Nutrition: Calories: 102.2; Fat: 3.9 g; Protein: 12.5 g; Carbs: 2.7 g; Fibre: 0 g; Sugar: 0 g

SIMPLE SALMON

5 minutes

20-25 minutes

4

INGREDIENTS

- 4 salmon filets
- 3 lemons
- 8 sprigs rosemary
- 1 Tablespoon olive oil
- Salt

DIRECTIONS

1   Slice the lemons into thin slices.
2   Place several lemon slices on the bottom of the Air Fryer basket.
3   Now lay 4 rosemary sprigs on the lemons.
4   Arrange one salmon filet on top of each sprig of rosemary. Sprinkle some salt on the salmon.
5   Top each salmon filet with another sprig of rosemary. Cover with more lemon slices.
6   Drizzle with the olive oil on top.
7   Put the fry basket in the fryer. Set the temperature to 135°C. Set the timer for 20 minutes.
8   Take a fork and check the salmon, If it flakes easily, it's ready. If not, it needs 5 minutes more.
9   Serve the salmon with roasted lemon slices and rosemary.

Nutrition: Calories: 242; Fat: 12 g; Protein: 29 g; Carbs: 0 g; Fibre: 0 g; Sugar: 0 g

CHAPTER 6: DESSERTS

FRIED BANANAS WITH CHOCOLATE SAUCE

 10 minutes

 10 minutes

 3

INGREDIENTS

- 1 large egg
- 30 g corn flour
- 30 g plain breadcrumbs
- 3 bananas halved crosswise
- Cooking oil
- Chocolate sauce

DIRECTIONS

1. In a small bowl, beat the egg. In another bowl, place the corn flour.
2. Place the breadcrumbs in a third bowl.
3. Dip the bananas in the corn flour, then the egg, and then the breadcrumbs.
4. Spray the air fryer basket with cooking oil. Place the bananas in the basket and spray them with cooking oil.
5. Set temperature to 180°C (360°F) and cook for 5 min. Open the air fryer and flip the bananas—Cook for an additional 2 min. Transfer the bananas to plates.
6. Drizzle the chocolate sauce over the bananas and serve.
7. You can make your chocolate sauce using two tbsp milk and 30 g chocolate chips. Heat a saucepan over medium-high heat. Add the milk and stir for 1 to 2 min. Add the chocolate chips. Stir for 2 min, or until the chocolate has melted.

Nutrition: Calories: 20; Fat: 6g; Protein: 3g; Fibre: 3g

CREAMY CHOCOLATE ECLAIRS

15 minutes

25 minutes

9

INGREDIENTS

Éclair Dough:
- 50 g Butter
- 100 g Plain Flour
- 3 Medium Eggs
- 150 ml Water

Cream Filling:
- 1 tsp. Vanilla Essence
- 1 tsp. Icing Sugar
- 150 ml Whipped Cream

Chocolate Topping:
- 50 g Milk chocolate (chopped into chunks)
- 1 tbsp. Whipped Cream
- 25 g Butter

DIRECTIONS

1. Preheat the Air Fryer to 180°C.
2. While it is heating up, place the butter in the water, melt over medium heat, using a large pan, then bring to the boil.
3. Now remove it from the heat and stir in the flour.
4. Place the pan again to the heat and stir into it forms a medium ball in the middle of the pan.
5. Transfer the dough to a cold plate so that it can cool. Once it is cool beat in the eggs until you have a smooth mixture.
6. Then make into éclair shapes and place in the Air Fryer. Cook for 10 minutes on 180°C and a further 8 minutes on 160°C.
7. While the dough is cooking make your cream filling: Mix with a whisk the whipped cream, vanilla essence and icing sugar until nice and thick.
8. Leave the eclairs to cool and while they are cooling make your chocolate topping – Place the milk chocolate, whipped cream and butter into a glass bowl. Place it over a pan of hot water and mix well until you have melted chocolate.
9. Cover the tops of the eclairs with melted chocolate and then serve!

Nutrition: Calories: 181; Fat: 13 g; Protein: 4 g; Carbs: 27.5 g; Fibre: 1.5 g; Sugar: 3 g

GINGER BISCUITS

10 minutes

16 minutes

10-12

INGREDIENTS

- 270 g plain flour
- 2 tsp ground ginger
- 2 tsp baking soda
- 1 tbsp cinnamon
- ½ tsp salt
- 170 g butter room temperature
- 200 g white sugar
- 1 egg
- 85 g maple syrup
- 70 g sugar for coating the cookies

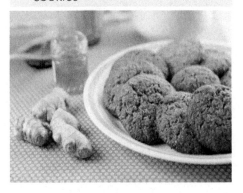

DIRECTIONS

1. In a large bowl, mix together the flour, ginger, baking soda, cinnamon, and salt.
2. In a second bowl, beat the butter with the sugar, egg, and maple syrup until creamy.
3. Combine the dry ingredients with the wet ones. Once everything is mixed, shape into small balls using your hands.
4. Flat each ball a little (the thicker the better!)
5. Preheat your air fryer at 150°C, and then air fry the cookies for 8 minutes at the same temperature.
6. Add 4-6 biscuits simultaneously (leaving space between each one). It is not necessary to rotate them.
7. Cook until hard on the outside but soft to touch when you press the biscuit.
8. Repeat steps 6-8 for the remaining cookies.
9. Let cool before eating and enjoy!

Nutrition: Calories 300; Fat 14 g; Protein 4 g; Carbs 45 g; Fibre 3 g; Sugar 25 g

CINNAMON ROLLS

5 minutes

10 minutes

6

INGREDIENTS

For The Rolls
- 2 tbsp. melted butter, plus more for brushing
- 75 g packed brown sugar
- 1/2 tsp. ground cinnamon
- Salt
- Plain flour, for surface
- 225 g ready rolled pizza dough

For The Glaze
- 50 g cream cheese, softened
- 65 g icing sugar
- 1 tbsp. whole milk, plus more if needed

DIRECTIONS

1. Prepare the rolls: Line the bottom of the fryer with parchment paper and brush with butter. In a medium bowl, mix together the butter, brown sugar, cinnamon, and a large pinch of salt until smooth and fluffy.
2. On a lightly floured surface, roll out the dough into one piece . Pinch the seams and fold them in half. Roll out to a 22cm x 18cm rectangle.
3. Spread the butter mixture over the dough, leaving a 1.5cm border. Roll up the dough starting on the long side, then cut crosswise into 6 pieces.
4. Place the pieces, cut-side up, evenly spaced in the air fryer basket.
5. Set the fryer to 180°C and air fry for about 10 minutes, until they are golden brown and cooked through.
6. Prepare the frosting: In a medium bowl, beat together the cream cheese, powdered sugar, and milk. If needed, add more milk using a teaspoon to thin the glaze.
7. Spread the glaze on warm cinnamon rolls and serve.

Nutrition: Calories: 251; Fat: 8 g; Protein: 3 g; Carbs: 39 g; Fibre: 0.5 g; Sugar: 22 g

CHOCOLATE AND CHILLI BROWNIES IN THE AIRFRYER

15 minutes

40 minutes

6

INGREDIENTS

- 200 g butter, melted
- 100 g cocoa powder
- 75 g dark chocolate, melted
- 2 large eggs
- 150 g caster sugar
- 1/2 tsp vanilla essence
- 150 g self-raising flour
- 1 level tbsp crushed dried chilli flakes

DIRECTIONS

1. Preheat the air fryer to 180°C
2. Mix the butter, sugar and crushed dried chillies.
3. Beat and mix in the eggs. Add the melted chocolate and vanilla essence.
4. Gradually add the flour and cocoa powder. Mix gently, do not stir too much.
5. Using a greased or baking paper lined tin/container, pour in the mixture.
6. Cook in the air fryer for 15 to 20 minutes, checking periodically to see if the upper part does not burn; If it's cooking quickly, cover it with foil or baking paper.
7. When it's done, let it cool, then cut into smaller portions to serve.

Nutrition: Calories: 300; Fat: 22 g; Protein: 5 g; Carbs: 19 g; Fibre: 5 g; Sugar: 11 g

FLUFFY BLUEBERRY FRITTERS

5 minutes

15 minutes

4

INGREDIENTS

- 95 g all-purpose flour
- 1 tsp baking powder
- 65 ml coconut milk
- 2 tbsp coconut sugar
- A pinch of sea salt
- 1 egg
- 2 tbsp melted butter
- 55 g fresh blueberries

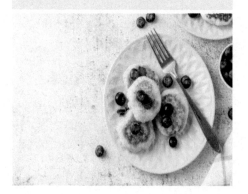

DIRECTIONS

1. In a mixing bowl, thoroughly mix all the ingredients.
2. Drop a spoonful of batter onto a greased Air Fryer pan. Cook in the preheated Air Fryer at 182°C (360°F) for 10 min, flipping halfway through the cooking time.
3. Repeat now with remaining batter and serve warm. Enjoy!

Nutrition: Calories: 195; Fat 8g; Carbs 25.4g; Protein 4.9 g; Sugars 6.9g; Fibre 1g

CHOCOLATE CHIP COOKIES

10 minutes

8 minutes

12

INGREDIENTS

- 115 g butter, melted
- 55 g brown sugar
- 50 g caster sugar
- 1 large egg
- 1 tsp. pure vanilla extract
- 185 g plain flour
- 1/2 tsp. bicarbonate of soda
- 1/2 tsp. salt
- 120 g chocolate chips
- 35 g chopped walnuts

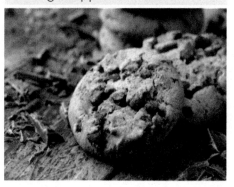

DIRECTIONS

1. In a medium bowl, combine melted butter and sugar. Add the egg and vanilla and beat until incorporated. Add the flour, baking soda, and salt and stir until combined.
2. Place a small piece of parchment in the frying basket, making sure there is room around the edges to allow air circulation. Working in batches, using a large cookie scoop (about 3 tablespoons), scoop the batter onto parchment paper, leaving 5 cm between each cookie. Press down the batter until slightly flattened.
3. Air fry for 8 minutes at 180 °C. The cookies will turn golden brown and slightly soft.
4. Let cool for 5 minutes before serving.

Nutrition: Calories: 220; Fat: 12 g; Protein: 3 g; Carbs: 24 g; Fibre: 2.5 g; Sugar: 11 g

SHORTBREAD CHOCOLATE BALLS

4 minutes

13 minutes

9

INGREDIENTS

- 175 g Butter
- 75 g Caster Sugar
- 250 g Plain Flour
- 1 tsp. Vanilla Essence
- 9 Chocolate chunks
- 2 tbsp. Cocoa

DIRECTIONS

1. Preheat your Air Fryer to 180°C.
2. Take a bowl and mix your sugar, flour, and cocoa.
3. Rub in the butter, knead well until you see a smooth dough.
4. Now divide into balls, place a chunk of chocolate into the centre of each one, make sure none of the chocolate chunk is showing.
5. Place your chocolate shortbread balls onto a baking sheet in your Air Fryer. Cook them at 180°C for 8 minutes and then a further 5 minutes on 160°C so that you can make sure they are cooked in the middle.
6. Serve!

Nutrition: Calories: 297; Fat: 18 g; Protein: 4 g; Carbs: 31 g; Fibre: 3.5 g; Sugar: 10 g

APRICOT AND RAISIN CAKE

10 minutes

12 minutes

8

INGREDIENTS

- 75g dried apricots, (just under 1/2 cup)
- 4 tbsp orange juice
- 75g self-raising flour, (3/4 cup)
- 40 g Sugar, (1/3 cup)
- 1 egg
- 75g Raisins, (just under 1/2 a cup)

DIRECTIONS

1. Preheat air fryer to 160°C
2. In a blender or food processor, puree the dried apricots and juices until smooth.
3. Put sugar and cake flour in another bowl and mix. Add a beaten egg to flour and sugar and mix together. Add apricot puree and raisins and keep mixing.
4. Spray a small amount of oil on a baking pan suitable for the air fryers. Transfer and flatten the mixture in it.
5. Cook in the air fryer for 12 minutes and check after 10 minutes. Use a metal skewer to check if it is done. If desired, return the cake to the air fryer and brown for a few more minutes.
6. Allow to cool, then remove from pan and slice.

Nutrition: Calories: 116; Fat: 1 g; Carbohydrates: 26 g; Fibre: 1 g; Sugar: 16 g; Protein: 2 g

MINI APPLE PIE

5 minutes

18 minutes

9

INGREDIENTS

- 75 g Plain Flour
- 33 g Butter
- 15 g Caster Sugar
- Water
- 2 Medium Red Apples
- Pinch Cinnamon
- Pinch Caster Sugar

DIRECTIONS

1. Preheat your Air Fryer to 180°C.
2. Start by making your pastry – place the plain flour and butter in a mixing bowl and rub the fat into the flour. Add the sugar and mix well. Add the water until the ingredients are moist enough to combine into a nice dough. Knead the dough well until it has a smooth texture.
3. Cover your pastry tins with butter to stop it sticking and then roll out the pastry and fill your pastry tins.
4. Peel, dice your apples, place in the tins. Sprinkle them with sugar and cinnamon.
5. Add an extra pastry layer to the top and make some fork markings so that they can breathe.
6. Cook in the Air Fryer for 18 minutes.

Nutrition: Calories: 85; Fat: 3 g; Protein: 1 g; Carbs: 13.5 g; Fibre: 1.5 g; Sugar: 6.5 g

INDEX

CREDITS

Icon made by Pixel perfect from www.flaticon.com

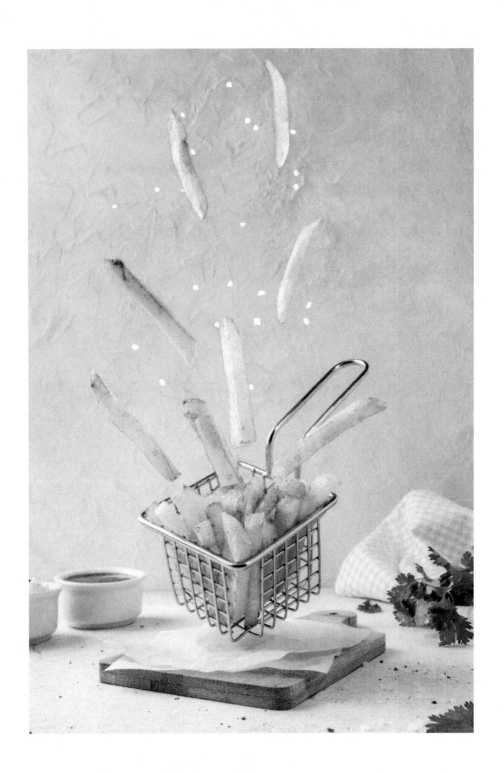

Printed in Great Britain
by Amazon

15521752R00045